D1320759

2100053192

E.L.R.S.

PANORAMA
A HISTORY *OF*
ROAD TRANSPORT
FROM CHARIOTS *TO* CADILLACS

Series designer: David Salariya
Editor: Penny Clarke
Artists: David Antram
Gordon Davies
James Field
Tony Townsend
Gerald Wood
John York

Illustrations by:
David Antram 20-21, 22-23, 36-37; **Gordon Davies** 30-31, 32-33; **James Field** 24-25; **Tony Townsend** 28-29, 34-35, 38-39, 42-43; **Gerald Wood** 8-9, 10-11, 12-13, 14-15, 16-17, 18-19, 26-27; **John York** 40-41.

First published in 1995
by Macdonald Young Books
Campus 400
Maylands Avenue
Hemel Hempstead
Herts HP2 7EZ

ISBN 0-7500-1587-X

© The Salariya Book Co Ltd MCMXCV

All rights reserved. No part of this book may be reproduced, stored in a retrieval system, or transmitted in any form or by any means, electronic, mechanical, photocopying, recording or otherwise, without the prior permission of the copyright owner.

Printed in Hong Kong by Paramount Printing Co. Ltd.

A CIP catalogue record for this book is available from the British Library.

Author:
Andrew Nahum is a curator at the Science Museum, London. He has written extensively on transport subjects. His books include *The Rotary Aero Engine* (HMSO, 1987) and *Alec Issigonis* (Design Council, 1988).

Series designer:
David Salariya was born in Dundee, Scotland, where he studied illustration and printmaking, concentrating on book design in his post-graduate year. He later completed a further post-graduate course in art education at Sussex University. He has illustrated a wide range of books on botanical, historical and mythical subjects. He has designed and created many new series of children's books for publishers in the UK and overseas, including the award-winning **Inside Story** series for Simon & Schuster. He lives in Brighton with his wife, the illustrator Shirley Willis.

PANORAMA

A HISTORY OF

ROAD TRANSPORT

FROM CHARIOTS TO CADILLACS

Written by
ANDREW NAHUM

Created & Designed by
DAVID SALARIYA

MACDONALD YOUNG BOOKS

S 351040

629.1 (E)

Contents

INTRODUCTION

For most of recorded history people built their homes from local materials and lived on local crops. Only valuable items, such as spices, salt and gold, were worth transporting. However, almost all business depends on transport and the history of wheeled vehicles is part of the history of transport and trade. Long before the train or the truck, huge quantities of metals, textiles and other goods were being drawn slowly but steadily by horses or other draught animals across the countries of the world.

More trade means more traffic, but there's nothing new about traffic jams. Photographs of

any of the world's major cities taken in the late 19th century show an almost solid mass of carts, private carriages, horse buses and cabs. Should traffic be allowed to increase? 'Greens' argue that, for the sake of the planet, it must not, even if that slows economic growth, but most people want their standard of living to improve.

There seems to be only one way out. When phone lines become 'information superhighways' and powerful computers at home amalgamate with the telephone and TV, many people will never need to leave home to work or to meet. Perhaps you will have friends that you only meet on a screen. If that seems unlikely, remember that a Roman charioteer would have thought a wheeled vehicle on the moon just as unlikely!

2500 BC

2500 BC

THE ANCIENT WORLD

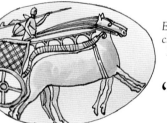

Engraving of chariot, Crete, 1400 BC.

Jointed Egyptian horse-bit made of bronze, c1200 BC.

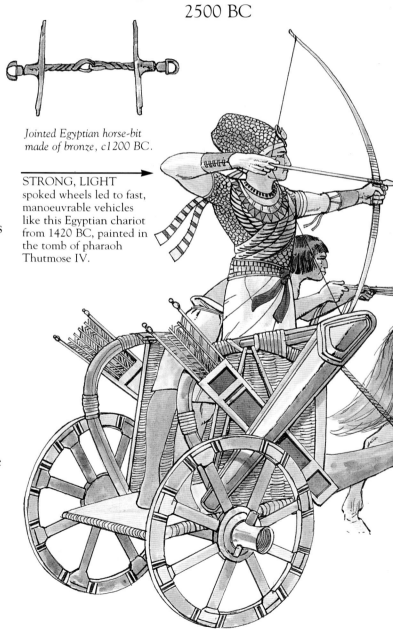

STRONG, LIGHT spoked wheels led to fast, manoeuvrable vehicles like this Egyptian chariot from 1420 BC, painted in the tomb of pharaoh Thutmose IV.

'It's as old as the wheel' is an old saying. But how old is that? Wheeled vehicles were relatively late inventions. Tools, pottery and the skill to melt and cast bronze were all in use long before wheeled vehicles.

Carts dating from about 5,000 years ago (3000 BC) have been found in Sumeria (part of present-day Iraq) – an area often called 'the cradle of civilization'. Archaeological discoveries suggest that the earliest carts were used for the funerals of important people. Later, they were probably used to haul grain and agricultural produce to the cities. Oxen, or sometimes onagers (a type of wild ass), pulled them.

Early vehicles had solid disc wheels, often made from three pieces of wood held together by crosswise wooden braces. Around 2000 BC the spoked wheel was developed in the Middle East. This was far lighter and had a natural springiness, which helped it resist shocks. At about the same time the horse was domesticated. Together, horses and spoked wheels led to speedy and manoeuvrable war chariots. These were the army tanks of their day.

Outside the few cities, roads were just rough tracks and few people made long journeys.

900 BC

2500 BC

1900 BC

540 BC 300 BC

EGYPTIAN wheelwrights at work, from a tomb-painting at Thebes, c1500 BC. Some of the wheels discovered in ancient Egyptian tombs were made of imported elm.

WHEELED TRANSPORT may have developed from the potter's wheel. This example was drawn on an Egyptian tomb in about 1800 BC. Sadly, there is no record of who first thought of making this single horizontal rotating wheel upright and using it in pairs for transport.

'CROSS-BAR' spoked wheel from Mercurago in northern Italy, c1000 BC. Like the later wheel from Greece (top right), it seems to be midway between a solid wheel and a spoked wheel with a central hub, like those on the Egyptian chariot (left). The main spoke in this wheel was made of walnut.

HORSES FROM AN Assyrian frieze, c850 BC. They have elaborate bridles and are controlled with a bit in the mouth.

2500 BC Ox cart with a wicker body from Susa, Iran. Like most early wheeled vehicles this has solid disc wheels built up from three pieces of timber.

2500 BC Two-wheeled cart shown in a limestone carving from the ancient city of Ur in Mesopotamia (part of present-day Iraq). It is drawn by onagers.

2500 BC Four-wheeled war chariots from Ur. No one knows quite how these early disc wheels worked. Did they rotate on the end of the axle (like the wheels of the cart on page 11), or were they fixed rigidly to the axle so that both axle and wheels turned together?

1900 BC Egyptian pack-ass. Pack animals were more convenient than carts for carrying light loads. They could go where the ground was too rough or muddy for wheeled vehicles.

900 BC An Assyrian hunting chariot, a carving from the tomb of Ashurnasirpal, Nimrud, Mesopotamia.

540 BC Greek country cart with 'cross-bar' spoked wheels. A single 'master spoke' crosses the diameter of the wheel. The four other spokes are notched into it, and not into a central hub.

300 BC Greek military chariot pulled by a pair of horses. The open body gave little protection to those in the chariot, but made it very light, which meant it could travel much more swiftly.

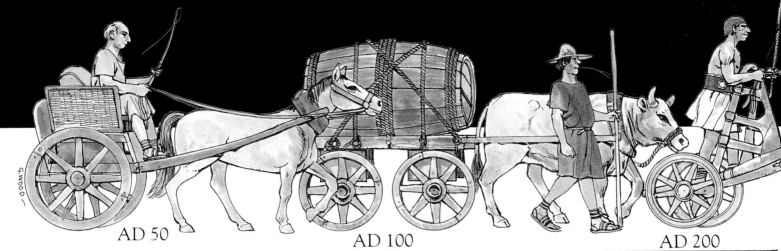

AD 50　　　　　　　AD 100　　　　　　　AD 200

THE ROMANS

Boy's chariot, 3rd century AD. The horse is between a pair of wooden shafts, a new style of harness.

The Romans built a network of magnificent roads across their empire. They would dig broad trenches, which they filled with carefully graded layers of different materials. These ranged from fine sand at the bottom to larger stones or cobbles on the surface. Some of the most important roads around Rome were paved with stone slabs. Slabs and cobbles made a hard surface that was easier for the oxen or horses pulling carts and waggons, though the noise of the wheels on the stone must have been dreadful. Most roads, however, were surfaced with small stones or gravel.

A good network of roads was important, for it allowed the government in Rome to control its huge empire. The roads meant that marching soldiers or government messengers on horseback could travel rapidly, whatever the weather.

The Romans used a wide range of vehicles. For example slow and heavy ox waggons (*clabularia*) could each carry about 500 kilos of army goods and needed eight oxen (or ten in winter when the roads were muddy). Other vehicles are shown in the frieze across the top of the page.

In spite of the magnificent engineering of their roads and bridges the Romans did not harness their animals efficiently. The high collar of the harness restricted an ox's or a horse's breathing.

Celtic waggon from Hallstat, Austria, c500 BC. It was probably made in France or Germany by Celtic craftsmen and imported for an important funeral.

THE MAIN ROADS of Italy, c200 BC. The most important, like the Via Appia or the Via Flaminia, were paved with blocks of stone.

FOUR-WHEELED travelling waggon, cAD 200. An example of a high collar which would have limited the horse's pulling power.

AD 300

AD 380

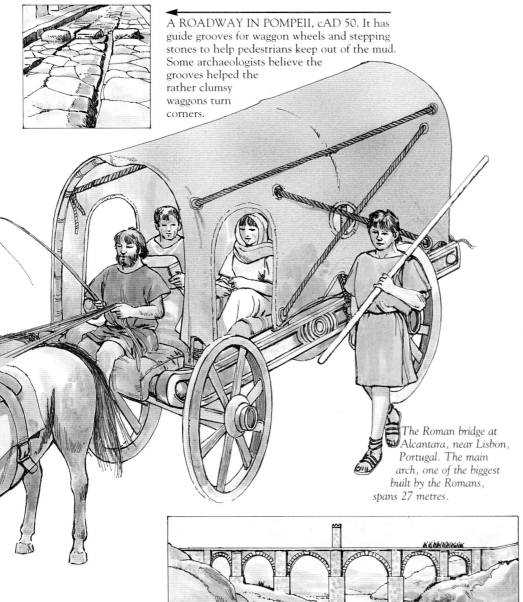

A ROADWAY IN POMPEII, cAD 50. It has guide grooves for waggon wheels and stepping stones to help pedestrians keep out of the mud. Some archaeologists believe the grooves helped the rather clumsy waggons turn corners.

The Roman bridge at Alcantara, near Lisbon, Portugal. The main arch, one of the biggest built by the Romans, spans 27 metres.

AD 50 Two-wheeled passenger cart, or *cisium*, pulled by a single horse.

AD 100 A freight waggon, or *plaustrum*, hauled by an ox. It is carrying a barrel of wine. Like the horse pulling the *cisium*, the ox has a collar round its throat. But it is not controlled with reins, just a rope around its nose.

AD 200 Roman war chariot. These fast, light chariots gave the Romans a great advantage over their enemies. Another type of Roman war chariot, the *quadriga*, was drawn by four horses. Chariot racing was a very popular sport and was a highlight of the games that took place each year to celebrate events such as the emperor's birthday.

AD 300 Farm cart. Progress is not always consistent. Solid disc wheels were still used for thousands of years after spoked wheels had been invented: largely because they were easier, and so cheaper, to make.

AD 380 A four-wheeled public coach in which poorer people could travel from town to town. The horses pulling it have breaststraps fitted between their front legs and around their bodies. The straps helped reduce the choking effect of the collar which pressed on a horse's throat when it was pulling a cart or waggon. The heavier the load the horse had to pull, the harder the collar pressed on its throat and the more difficult it was for the horse to breathe and pull the load.

210 BC   100 BC

The Dark Ages

Early iron stirrups, found in Hungary. They were probably brought there by horsemen from Central Asia in about AD 560.

Paying for roads was (and is) a problem. In the Roman Empire citizens were often forced to maintain the roads in their area. They were also expected to provide feed for horses taking traffic on government business. This was expensive and some government officials abused the system. By about AD 350, the Roman Empire was beginning to decline, and as it did so the great road system declined with it.

As the road system broke down, so harnesses improved. From about AD 900 a properly proportioned horse collar was used in western Europe. This allowed a horse to pull a greater load, for a well-designed and padded collar rests on the animal's shoulders and does not press on the windpipe and obstruct breathing like earlier types.

Nomadic peoples in Asia developed horse riding from about 1000 BC, and cavalry had gradually replaced chariots in war. However, here too, better harness was needed. Although stirrups were known in China in AD 470, they were not adopted generally in Europe until after about AD 700. They made it far easier to stay on a horse, and riding probably grew in popularity as the decaying Roman roads became more difficult for wheeled traffic to use.

VIKING CART from the Oseberg burial, near Oslo, Norway, cAD 850. The Vikings believed that the dead person should be able to travel by land or sea, although it is unlikely that wheeled transport was much use in mountainous Norway.

Viking sledge, cAD 850. Unlike the Oseberg cart, the sledges also found in the burial mound seem to have been built for use – their runners show signs of wear.

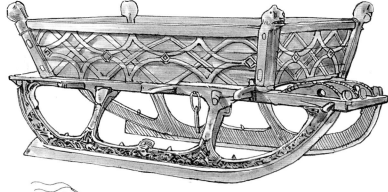

A 10TH-CENTURY French cart with wooden shafts and collars for the horses.

100 BC

AD 600

THE WHEELS of the cart are crudely made – unlike the light Celtic or Roman wheels (above right and on page 11). The decorative carving on the front and sides of the cart is very fine, indicating that it was to be used by an important person.

210 BC Archaeological evidence shows that Chinese roads were often better than Roman ones. Between 1100 and 200 BC a massive network of roads was built throughout China. Many were just narrow tracks, but others were highways with special lanes for important traffic. However, from around AD 300 China's roads fell into disuse and decline, just as the Romans' did at much the same time. This is a reconstruction of the wooden chariots found in a tomb in northern China where the famous 'army' of terracotta soldiers was also found.

100 BC Bronze model of a covered Chinese vehicle, discovered by archaeologists in 1980.

100 BC Celtic ceremonial carriage discovered in a burial in a peat-bog at Dejbjerg in southern Denmark in 1881. The bog had helped to preserve the carriage because it prevented oxygen, which causes decay, reaching the burial. The carriage has a single, central shaft to which the two oxen pulling it were harnessed. The sides of the carriage are carved, another indication that it was not an ordinary farm vehicle.

AD 600 Chinese horse with saddle and stirrups. Stirrups help riders keep their balance, so making horses easier to ride. They were probably first made by Chinese smiths sometime during the 5th century AD.

BYZANTINE WAR CHARIOTS, 9th century AD. The horse collar had been widely adopted in western Europe by this time. But in the Byzantine Empire (the eastern part of the old Roman Empire), harnesses with breaststraps, like those that the Romans had used, were still in widespread use.

1300

1317

THE MIDDLE AGES

A Saxon woodcutter with a two-wheeled cart, 11th century. The rim of the wheel is made of several parts (felloes).

During the Middle Ages, vehicles in Europe did not change much. Increasing use of the padded horse collar and iron horseshoes enabled animals to work more efficiently and pull greater loads. Smaller carts could now use a single horse, instead of two animals harnessed side by side, because the collar, attached to a pair of shafts on the cart, made better use of the animal's power.

Passenger vehicles were still basically unsprung covered carts. It is not known exactly who used them or what the average journey might have been. Certainly the coaches were uncomfortable so most people would not have chosen to travel that way unless they were lame or unwell. Messengers on government business rode on horseback, as did private travellers who were rich enough to keep a horse.

Haulage firms existed, like today, and packages or loads could be sent to a destination hundreds of kilometres away, with reasonable certainty that they would arrive. Some merchants rode on horseback, leading a string of packhorses with them. Such transport was expensive and was mainly used for relatively high-value items like spices, silk, and small metal items like buckles and fastenings for clothing.

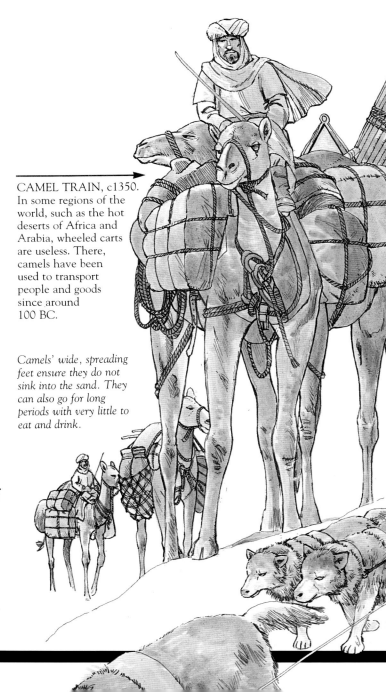

CAMEL TRAIN, c1350. In some regions of the world, such as the hot deserts of Africa and Arabia, wheeled carts are useless. There, camels have been used to transport people and goods since around 100 BC.

Camels' wide, spreading feet ensure they do not sink into the sand. They can also go for long periods with very little to eat and drink.

1460

1460

A TWO-WHEELED CART, 13th century. Hurdles, woven basket-work frames, have been slotted into place to increase the height of the sides so the cart can carry a bigger load.

Inuit sledge and dog team, c1400. The Inuit (or Eskimo) culture is ancient and has a complex technology well adapted to the harsh Arctic environment.

METAL AND TIMBER were scarce, so the Inuit used animal bones instead. Sledges had bone runners, and weapons, such as spears, had tips of sharpened bone. Everything was lashed in place with animal tendons which made tough natural fastenings.

1300 A two-wheeled cart with studded wheels, carrying sheaves of corn. Strong, flexible, close-grained woods like ash, willow, poplar and elm were used for the felloes from which the wheel rims were made. The iron studs were a simple way of protecting the wooden wheel rim against wear. Using tyres, continuous hoops of iron, was better, but they were harder to make and fit. The rear horse is harnessed between shafts (a pair of wooden poles) while ropes run forward to the collars of the two horses in front.

1317 French travelling carriage. These carriages were unsprung, so passengers felt every bump from stones or ruts in the road. They were also very slow. The two horses pulling the carriage are controlled by the postillion, the man riding the rear one.

1460 French baggage waggon. Two horses are pulling in tandem. The rear horse is pulling between shafts to which the front horse is linked by chains. A leather strap, known as the crupper, is fixed to the saddle and loops under the horse's tail. This helps to keep the saddle in place.

1460 A porter using a wheelbarrow to carry a travelling trunk. This simple 'vehicle' does not seem to have been used in Europe in earlier periods. Clearly, it was only practical for very short 'journeys' in towns and cities.

1500

1556

THE 16TH CENTURY

Miner using a wheelbarrow to transport freshly-mined metal ore, 16th century.

In the 16th century there was a great upsurge in manufacturing and trade in Europe. Mining, metal-working and textile manufacture all began to increase and so did people's prosperity.

Historians used to think that poor roads meant wheeled vehicles played little part in carrying goods at this time. They believed that most goods went by sea or river. New studies have shown this is not true. Stage waggons were pulled by large teams of horses which were changed for fresh ones at the end of each 'stage' or section of the route. They made slow but steady progress over long distances. Records show that major European ports, such as Southampton and Hamburg, sent regular loads by cart to most important cities inland.

The increase in trade and prosperity brought a need for more and better transport. The unsprung carriage of the early 16th century was gradually replaced by the coach. This had a body suspended by leather straps to give some cushioning from road shocks. The word 'coach' comes from Kocsi, the name of a town in Hungary, but it is not clear if straps for springing were really first used there.

▲ WHEELWRIGHT boring out the hub of a wheel, 1568. The wheelwright was an important member of the community, for only a well-made wheel had the strength and pliability to withstand the wrenching caused by poor roads. In the background an apprentice shapes wood for wheel spokes.

1560

1568

1570

1570

DUTCH TWO-WHEELED cart, 1627. The shafts run to a well-padded horse collar. The first shafts were rigidly attached to the vehicle. But by this period shafts were pivoted, making carts and carriages much more manoeuvrable.

PACKHORSE, c1550. Transporting goods by packhorse cost about 30 per cent more than by cart. Horses, however, were faster and could travel over poor roads and tracks where carts could not go.

NATIVE AMERICAN with horse and travois, a sliding load carrier. This method of transport is very ancient and is believed to have been used with dogs in North America, before Europeans introduced horses in the 16th century. Similar devices were used in the cattle-rearing parts of Africa and, until early this century, in hilly parts of Ireland and Europe.

1500 A whirlicote, a simple unsprung carriage used for public hire in England. The horses are harnessed beside each other and not in tandem (one behind the other) as they usually were in the Middle Ages.

1556 German horse-drawn sledge. Sledges were used to drag metal ore or stone along unmade tracks in quarries or mines. About this time the first wooden tracks were laid in mines and quarries and sledges gradually gave way to wheeled trucks which were easier for horses to pull.

1560 Pack-dogs were quite widely used in the mountainous districts of Germany and central Europe. Dogs could only carry small loads, so using them made economic sense only if the load was reasonably valuable – for example, gold or silver ore.

1568 German coach. The horses of this coach were controlled by the postillion, who rode on one of the horses. Horse-drawn vehicles could also be controlled by a driver sitting on the vehicle and using long reins to the horses.

1570 Wheelbarrow, a simple but effective form of transport over very short distances and in confined places, such as mines.

1570 Large-wheeled cart used by a brewery to transport barrels of ale.

1620   1696   1793

17TH AND 18TH CENTURIES

Sedan chair, 1650. The sedan chair was better sprung than a coach and could be squeezed through crowds.

At the beginning of the 17th century coaches did not have springs, only leather straps which supported the coach body, making it sway sickeningly as the vehicle lurched along rutted, pot-holed roads.

However, long-distance wheeled transport was provided by stage waggons. These big, clumsy vehicles hauled goods from town to town. They were very heavy and their wheels cut deep ruts in the roads. There were frequent complaints by other road-users. Gradually, as a result of laws and toll charges, carriers were forced to use broad wheels that did less damage.

France was one of the first countries to try to improve its roads. The *Corps des Ponts et Chaussées*, founded in 1716, was the world's first government-funded body of road engineers.

In Britain and America, Turnpike Trusts were started to maintain and improve long-distance roads. By 1750 the British turnpikes formed an extensive and well-connected network of new, level roads. Better designed coaches, with steel springs, allowed much greater speeds. Coach services were a triumph of organization. At the end of each 'stage' of a few miles, teams of fresh horses waited to replace the tired set.

COACHING INN, 18th century. The inn was an essential part of coach travel. While the horses were changed the passengers had a meal.

STAGE WAGGON, 1770. They could carry up to six tonnes over long distances. These waggons were usually pulled by eight horses, which were changed after each stage.

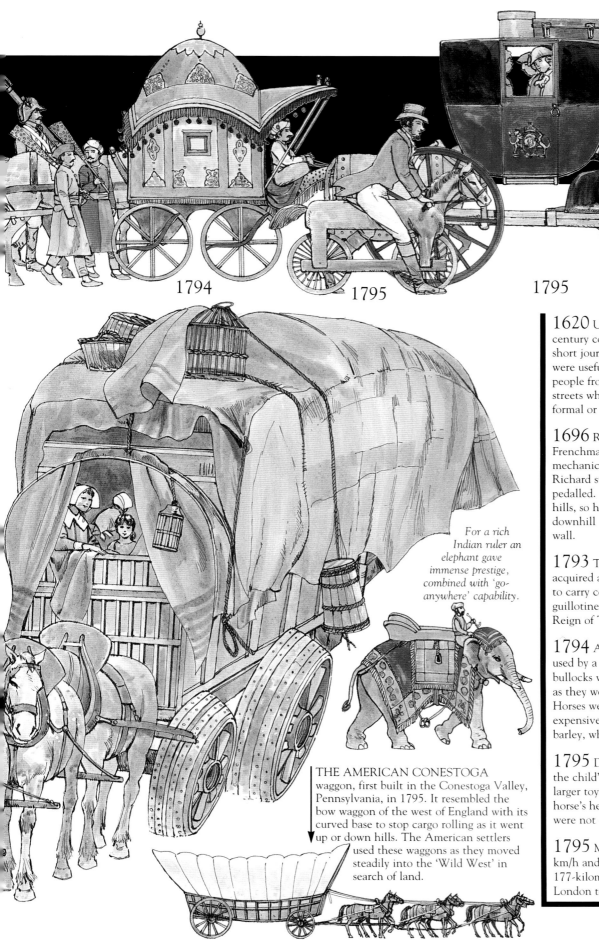

1794

1795

1795

For a rich Indian ruler an elephant gave immense prestige, combined with 'go-anywhere' capability.

THE AMERICAN CONESTOGA waggon, first built in the Conestoga Valley, Pennsylvania, in 1795. It resembled the bow waggon of the west of England with its curved base to stop cargo rolling as it went up or down hills. The American settlers used these waggons as they moved steadily into the 'Wild West' in search of land.

1620 Uncomfortable early 17th-century coaches were mostly used for short journeys in towns and cities. They were useful for protecting important people from the weather and muddy streets when they were on the way to formal or social occasions.

1696 Richard's Velocipede. A Frenchman, Dr Elie Richard, invented a mechanically propelled carriage. While Richard steered, his servant behind pedalled. It was too heavy to pedal up hills, so had to be pushed. Going downhill it ran away and crashed into a wall.

1793 The simple farm cart or tumbril acquired a sinister reputation: it was used to carry condemned aristocrats to the guillotine during the French Revolution's Reign of Terror in 1793.

1794 A decorated bullock cart or *rukh* used by a noble Indian lady. In India bullocks were the usual draught animals as they were tough and only ate hay. Horses were faster, but needed more expensive high-energy food, such as barley, wheat or oats.

1795 During the French Revolution the child's hobby-horse developed into a larger toy for grown-ups. Some still had a horse's head. Remarkably, the owners were not embarrassed to ride them.

1795 Mail coaches averaged 14-16 km/h and also carried passengers. The 177-kilometre journey from Bath to London took 16 hours.

1820

1828

EARLY TO MID 19TH CENTURY

In Paris, in 1818, Baron von Drais improved the hobby-horse. His two-wheeled velocipede was the ancestor of the bicycle.

'Prairie schooner', c1860. This was the nickname for the waggons of the American settlers who colonized the West.

The early 19th century was a time of great experiment in horse-drawn carriages and many new types were designed. Some used one horse, for economy. Others were designed for a pair, to give greater speed and range. Some, like the barouche, had face-to-face seating for sociability. Others were more dashing, and were favoured by fashionable gentlemen. Like motor vehicles today, there were specialized horse-drawn vehicles for almost every purpose.

The hobby-horse was transformed into the lighter velocipede. It must have been tiring to ride for it still lacked pedals and the rider pushed it along with his feet. The sight of a man riding a wheeled machine was still surprising and velocipede riders were a major attraction at fairs.

Steam made some false starts as a power source for road transport. In Paris Nicholas-Joseph Cugnot ran a steam vehicle in 1796. Joseph Bozek invented another in Prague in 1815, but it was not successful. Several other inventors tried to introduce steam passenger vehicles in the early 19th century. Some road authorities considered steam coaches a public nuisance and charged them toll fees up to ten times greater than those for horse-drawn carriages.

▲ SIMILAR to the Conestogas, but flatter, prairie schooners were hauled by up to ten oxen and could carry loads of three tonnes.

1833   1835   1839

THE ROCKAWAY,
1855. Many coaches in
America were derived
from European or English
styles. The Rockaway was
the first all-American
design and the first to give
the coachman protection
from the weather.

Dog cart, c1865. Dog
carts were originally
designed to carry an
owner and gun dog to
shooting parties.

An omnibus at
Islington Green,
London, 1848.
The first regular
horse omnibus
service in London
started in 1829,
running between
Paddington and the
City of London.

1820 A barouche, the most
fashionable open carriage of its day.
Well-to-do families used their barouches
for visiting friends or taking the air in the
park.

1820 The French velocipede was
adopted in England by Denis Johnson, a
coach-builder. He started a riding school
to promote his machines.

1828 Goldsworthy Gurney's steam
carriage. Three of Gurney's carriages
plied between Cheltenham and
Gloucester in 1831. Local opposition and
higher road tolls forced the service out of
business.

1833 Walter Hancock had better luck
with his steamers than Gurney. For a few
years a number of his vehicles ran a
regular passenger service round the City
of London.

1835 With the coming of the railways,
stage coaches fell into disuse. However,
affluent owners often kept an elegant
carriage and liked to show off their skills
at driving a 'four-in-hand' – a team of
four horses.

1839 The two-wheeled cabriolet was
considered very smart. As one owner
explained, it was 'a convenient vehicle
for unmarried men to go out in at night,
and return from either a dinner, or from
the theatre or opera. It saves the
inconvenience of a closed carriage, two
horsemen, a coachman and footman,
which involve a large amount of
expense'.

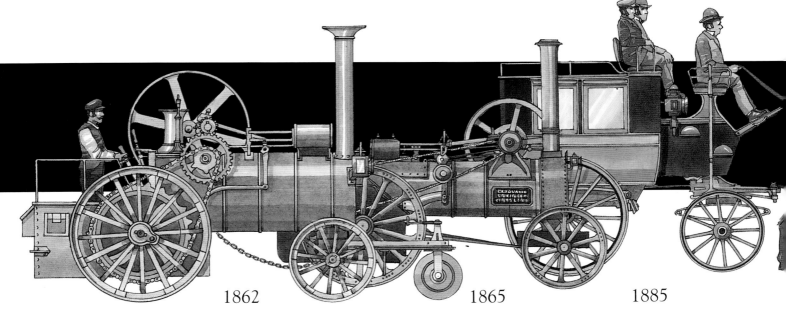

1862   1865   1885

STEAM AND CYCLES

Wooden-wheeled 'boneshaker' velocipede, 1870. The pedals were fixed to the front wheel spindle.

From about 1830, transport became increasingly mechanized. Though steam railways could reach remote places, steam did not take over on the roads due partly to the 'horse lobby'. For local journeys coaches and horses were still needed and the numbers in use grew.

We think of horse-drawn transport as romantic, but it had a grisly side. A draught horse survived, on average, less than two years. Every year the biggest knacker's yard in London slaughtered 26,000 animals that were no longer fit for work, and the situation was similar in other big cities throughout Europe and North America. Nothing was wasted. The hide went for leather, hooves were boiled down for glue, bones were ground for fertiliser and the flesh was sold for dogmeat or through cheap butchers.

There was also the problem of air pollution. A surgeon noted, 'The air in town in dry weather is loaded with dust, the greater part of which is dried and pulverized horse manure.'

Meanwhile the velocipede bicycle was becoming a serious means of transport. The fast, high-wheeled Ordinary appealed to sportsmen, but the Rover 'safety bicycle' was lower and made cycling a practical method of transport for anyone.

A velocipede riding school, 1869. Velocipede riding became popular in Europe and America, and schools were formed where riders could learn the new skill.

Ordinary rider, 1884. To make cycles faster, builders increased the size of the front wheel, creating the high Ordinary or 'Penny farthing'.

ORDINARY RIDERS, 1879. American bicycle pioneers in Massachusetts with their Ordinary machines meeting for the USA's first two-day cycling tour. A touring rider might travel at 16-19 km/h, but almost 32 km/h was possible for short distances.

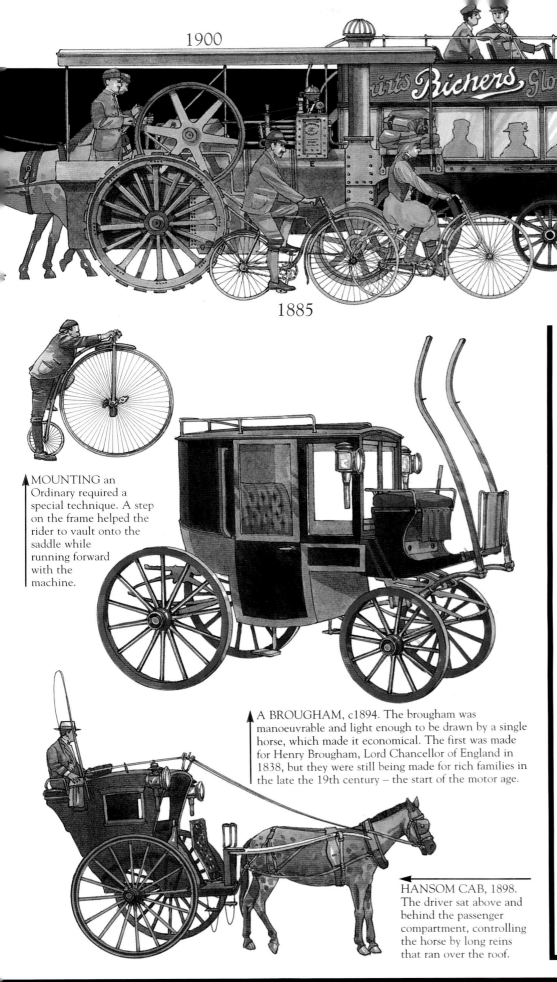

1900

1885

1905

MOUNTING an Ordinary required a special technique. A step on the frame helped the rider to vault onto the saddle while running forward with the machine.

A BROUGHAM, c1894. The brougham was manoeuvrable and light enough to be drawn by a single horse, which made it economical. The first was made for Henry Brougham, Lord Chancellor of England in 1838, but they were still being made for rich families in the late the 19th century – the start of the motor age.

HANSOM CAB, 1898. The driver sat above and behind the passenger compartment, controlling the horse by long reins that ran over the roof.

1862 Aveling traction engine. Steam railways increased rapidly from the 1830s, but steam road vehicles were resisted by those who feared they would frighten the horses. As a result, steam was reserved for powerful slow-moving traction engines used to pull heavy loads or to do agricultural work. In America, traction engines were more often used for farmwork, like threshing corn.

1865 Savage Traction Engine and Thresher. Many traction engines were owned by agricultural contractors who used the engine to tow their machinery from farm to farm. Once at the site the engine could pull a plough or drive machinery with a belt from the flywheel (the large wheel behind the chimney).

1885 Station bus. A rich country family might keep a special roomy coach such as this for meeting parties of guests arriving by train.

1885 John Kemp Starley's Rover 'Safety' bicycle used a newly developed chain and sprocket drive. This allowed it to reach speeds similar to those of modern bicycles without the high wheel of the Ordinary.

1900 Burrell traction engine going for shipment to South Africa for the Boer War (1899-1902). The traction engine had immense hauling power. One took a heavy field gun to the top of a 360-metre kop (hill) to overlook, and devastate, the Boers' positions.

1905 Horse-drawn bus. These buses survived into the 20th century, carrying shoppers and commuters even after motor transport was becoming common.

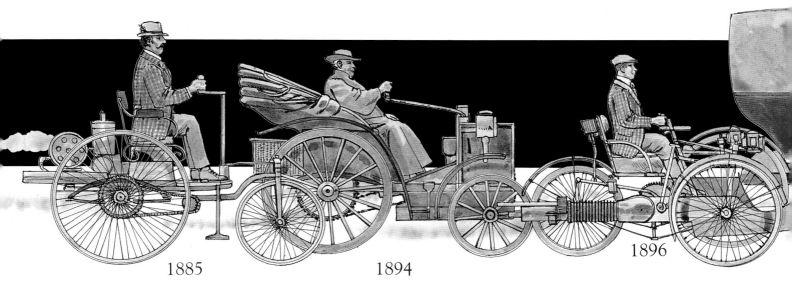

1885   1894   1896

INVENTION OF THE MOTOR CAR

Goggles and windproof coat for a Parisian poodle, 1903.

Some motoring garb was hideous, like this all-enveloping hood with transparent windows, but on early roads the dust could penetrate everywhere.

The ancestor of the petrol engine was the stationary gas engine, used from about 1880 to power machinery in small factories and workshops. They were lighter and simpler to run than steam engines, but still too heavy for a car or motorcycle. The German engineer Gottlieb Daimler (1834-1900) was one of the first engineers to lighten and miniaturize the gas engine for use in vehicles. He also adapted it to run on petrol – a convenient liquid fuel which could be stored in a tank. He ran his experimental motorcycle in 1885, following it the next year with a crude car. At the same time Karl Benz (1844-1929) was developing a petrol motor vehicle.

Most other industrialized countries quickly developed their own motor industries. France soon overtook Germany to become the main innovator and manufacturer in the years up to 1914.

Early cars were usually open, so motoring could be unpleasant. Dust was a problem in dry weather, and in wet weather occupants might be covered with muddy spray. Better windscreens and the use of tarred road surfaces reduced these problems.

WOMEN MOTORISTS who wished to wear a hat with a brim needed a generous hood or veil to go over it. However neater, closer headgear was more practical.

'CORRECT LIVERIES for the Chauffeur', as advertised by Drykitt Ltd of Oxford Street, London, in 1906. Owners who had bought fine cars wanted their chauffeurs to be smart too. An outfit consisting of jacket, breeches, leggings, gauntlet and cap, usually in muted blue, green or grey, cost £3 10s (£3.50).

Men's styles were simpler and some had fold-down goggles.

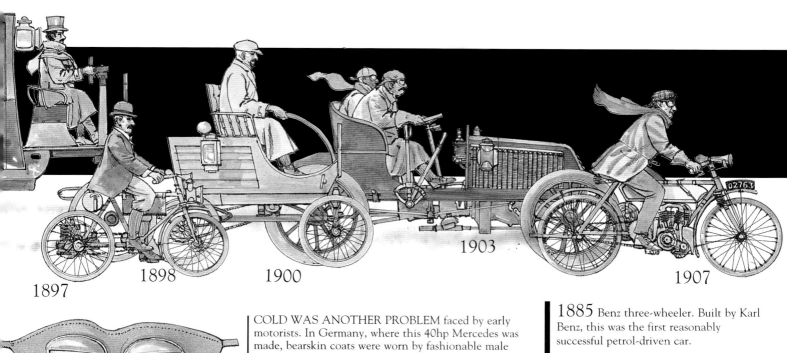

1897   1898   1900   1903   1907

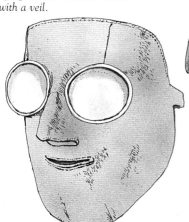

A facemask lined with soft kid leather, for the lady who feared the wind would ruin her complexion, 1911. An alternative, a pair of goggles (above), against grit and flying stones, could be worn with a veil.

COLD WAS ANOTHER PROBLEM faced by early motorists. In Germany, where this 40hp Mercedes was made, bearskin coats were worn by fashionable male motorists. Unfortunately such coats had their own problems. The fur held dust and became muddy in wet weather.

'MR NICHOLL OF REGENT STREET has the most charming spring coats eminently business-like and suitable for the purpose', noted *The Car* in 1902. For the new 'automobilists' it was important to be properly turned out. Motor publications had regular pages on fashion.

1885 Benz three-wheeler. Built by Karl Benz, this was the first reasonably successful petrol-driven car.

1894 The first practical cars were German, but the French quickly caught up. This is the sixth vehicle made by the Panhard & Levassor company in Paris. It was in use until 1928.

1896 Leon Bollée tricycle. This had a big single-cylinder engine, mounted low down and parallel to the ground. A Bollée averaged 45 km/h for over 62 kilometres in the 1897 Paris – Trouville race and could reach 50 km/h.

1897 Electric cabs operated by the London Electric Cab Company were the first mechanically-propelled taxis in Britain. The body was directly based on a four-wheeled, horse-drawn carriage.

1898 De Dion-Bouton tricycle. Count Albert de Dion (1856-1946), a wealthy French aristocrat, produced a light air-cooled petrol motor in association with the engineer Georges Bouton.

1900 Locomobile steam car. Steam cars were popular in the early days of motoring. Compared to contemporary petrol cars they were smooth, vibration-free and silent.

1903 Marcel Renault in the Paris – Madrid race, shortly before his fatal crash. In the early days, races were held on public roads and became a popular sport.

1907 By 1907 motorcycles were practical machines. This Norton won the first Isle of Man TT (Tourist Trophy) race at an average of 60 km/h.

1890

1897

Buses, Trams and Lorries

London tram c1902

The turn of the century, between 1890 and 1910, was a time of experiment. Horse transport was familiar and tested but horses were expensive to keep. New types of mechanical transport had economic appeal.

Steam was an obvious choice: it had been used in railway locomotives for many years. Steam buses, lorries and cars were all produced. But regulating the fire in the boiler and operating the engine controls needed knowledge and skill.

Electric vehicles were much simpler and their silence and lack of fumes were appreciated even then. However, like electric vehicles today, they needed heavy batteries, which made them slow. Then, every 80 or 95 kilometres the batteries needed recharging and that took 10 to 12 hours. Nevertheless, the Belgian racing driver Camille Jenatzy managed to reach 106 km/h over a short distance in 1899 with his electric car, *La Jamais Contente* – a world speed record. Electric trams, drawing their power from overhead cables, did not have the problem of battery recharging, and most cities developed a tramway network.

The most versatile power unit was the petrol engine. Though noisy and jerky in the early days, it used less fuel than the steam car, and had a far greater range than the electric car.

Traction engine and trailer laying tram rails. Trams provided energy-efficient public transport for commuters and shoppers.

BREWER'S STEAM waggon, 1906. The makers claimed these waggons could cover 16,000 kilometres in 15 months with only one day off for repairs. Right: The cab, with boiler, steam controls and steering wheel.

1902   1903   1906   1907

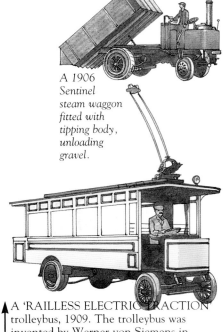

A 1906
Sentinel
steam waggon
fitted with
tipping body,
unloading
gravel.

A 'RAILLESS ELECTRIC TRACTION' trolleybus, 1909. The trolleybus was invented by Werner von Siemens in Berlin in 1882. It collected electric current from overhead wires, but there were no rails and the driver had to steer.

← LONDON B-TYPE omnibus, introduced in 1910. This petrol-powered bus was used for the first standardized bus fleet in the world.

Sentinel steam lorry, 1910, with a 4,500-litre tanker body for street cleaning.

1890 Horse-drawn tram. Trams ran on iron rails set into the road. A horse could haul twice as many people over smooth rails as on an ordinary road. The first tram line opened in New York in 1832. The first European trams started running in Paris in 1855.

1897 Bersey Humming Bird electric cab. Battery-electric powered vehicles seemed attractive in the early days of mechanical transport because they were simple to operate and their noise level was low. The Bersey electric cab could run for 80–95 kilometres at about 14 km/h on one charge. However, this range was too short to be economic and the service was not a financial success.

1902 Thorneycroft steam bus. This ran in London between Hammersmith and Oxford Circus in 1902. It was basically a steam lorry fitted with a body used on horse buses.

1903 American Fischer petrol-electric bus. Today, hybrid diesel-electric power is being researched again by major car makers, such as Volkswagen in Germany, to reduce urban pollution.

1906 Sentinel waggon. Steam engines vied with petrol engines for haulage of goods and heavy loads at the turn of the century. Steam waggons like this were durable and effective. However, the driver had to build a fire to get up steam in the boiler each morning and the petrol (or later the diesel) lorry took over, thanks to quicker starting, better fuel consumption and easier driving.

1907 Petrol-powered Daimler commercial van.

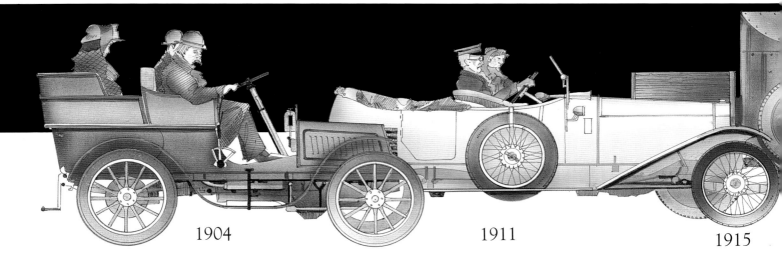

1904   1911   1915

ROLLS-ROYCE AND HENRY FORD

Henry Royce (1863-1933). Brought up in poverty with little education, Royce was determined to be a successful engineer.

Henry Ford (1863-1947) and Henry Royce (1863-1933) were each typical of their age and their countries. Ford, in the USA, wanted quantity production and low prices. He dreamed of a car for all that could be made really cheaply because it was simple and standardized. He realized that a moving assembly line, in which cars moved past the workers, was more efficient than a factory where the workers had to move from one place to another for different tasks and where the partly assembled cars had to be moved about by hand. Politicians and industrialists travelled to see Ford's Detroit factories where steel and parts poured in at one end and finished cars came out in huge numbers at the other. His system of factory organization got a name of its own: 'Fordism'.

By contrast Royce aimed for superb quality. His production did not depend on moving assembly lines and automatic machines, but on the skills of the finest British engineers and fitters. He met Charlie Rolls in 1904. Rolls moved in privileged social circles where he sold expensive cars. He imported French Panhard and Belgian Minerva cars, but wanted a British product, and encouraged Royce to build bigger, smoother cars. These became known as Rolls-Royces.

The Honourable C S 'Charlie' Rolls, 1877-1910, was an early ballooning, motoring, gliding and flying enthusiast, and one of the first people in Britain to learn to fly.

Rolls combining his two passions: he uses his Rolls-Royce to tow a glider to its launch point, 1909.

THE TYPE 70 Rolls-Royce, a powerful 6-cylinder, 7-litre car, on its way to winning a Gold Medal for reliability and performance in the RAC's 3,218-kilometre Scottish Trial in 1908.

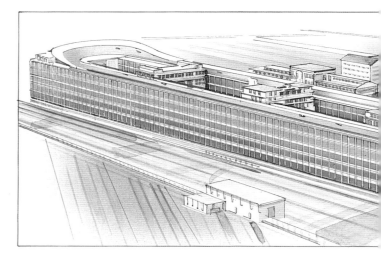

1915

1916

1917

1917

THE FAMOUS FORD Model T. By 1918 half the world's cars were Ford Model Ts. Fifteen million were built between 1908 and 1927.

THE AMERICAN car manufacturer Henry Ford (1863-1947) was, like Royce, a self-made man. He, too, had started from humble beginnings and had taught himself engineering.

1904 The first car made by Henry Royce, based on the French-built Decauville he owned.

1911 The London-to-Edinburgh Rolls-Royce. This was specially made for a public trial, promoted by the company, to prove its speed and endurance by driving from London to Edinburgh in top gear. It achieved a fuel consumption of 8 km/litre on the run and was later timed at a top speed of 125 km/h at Brooklands racetrack in Surrey.

1915 Rolls-Royce armoured car. During the war Rolls-Royce Silver Ghost cars were fitted with armour and a machine gun.

1915 Royal Enfield motorcycle and sidecar, adapted as a mobile machine-gun unit.

1916 The Rolls-Royce Silver Ghost offered speed and unrivalled reliability for the time. Many were used in World War One as communications and staff cars.

1917 Model H Triumph. At the outbreak of war in 1914 the military authorities chose the two best standard motorcycles that had been produced for the 1914 season: the Triumph and the Douglas. The Triumph featured a sturdy iron single-cylinder engine driving a three-speed gearbox by a chain.

1917 Open versions of the Rolls-Royce Silver Ghost were also used as staff cars. They were so reliable that when King George V and Queen Mary visited the battle zone in France they used a Rolls-Royce instead of their usual Daimler.

EXPORTING FORDISM. The Italian car company Fiat's vast Lingotto factory in Turin. Building work began in 1916 and brought American techniques to European car-making. The roof-top test-track was an Italian touch.

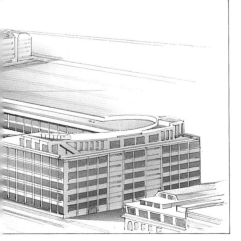

'A modern wonder of the world': Ford's Detroit factory, opened in 1910 to build the Ford Model T.

The first Ford moving production line, 1913. It was used to assemble ignition equipment.

Elegant spiral ramps linked the production floors of the Fiat factory at Lingotto in Italy.

Fiat 501s coming off the assembly line at Lingotto, 1924. Ford's methods were widely copied.

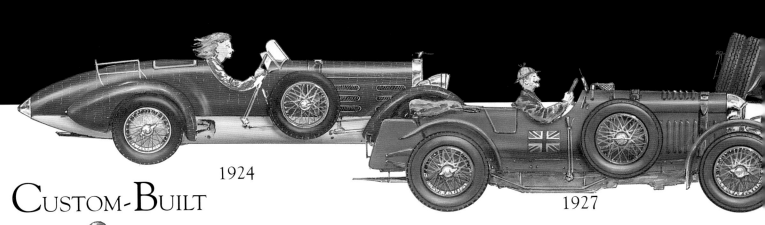

1924

1927

CUSTOM-BUILT

Douglas twin-cylinder motorcycle, 1920. Prince Albert (later King George VI) rode one.

The 1920s and 1930s were the great age of custom-built motor cars, when makers sent the 'rolling chassis', with all the mechanical parts in place, to a specialized body maker. These craftsmen were called coach-builders because they used many building techniques developed in the age of horse-drawn vehicles. They made a body of hand-beaten aluminium to the customer's design.

Traditional coach-building methods allowed small production runs and special 'one-off' bodies. The death-knell of the craft came with machine-pressed steel body panels. In 1916 the American Edward Budd built 70,000 cars for Dodge using the new technique. Steel replaced aluminium for ease of welding and strength. To show the strength of cars built by his system, Budd had a 5-tonne elephant stand on the roof of a Chrysler, while the doors continued to open and close normally. By 1928 half of all car bodies in the US were welded steel.

The technique spread only slowly into Europe where the market for cars was smaller. The tools for the new method were expensive, so the makers had to sell many more of the same model to make the change worthwhile. However, by 1934 André Citröen imported Budd techniques to build his famous *traction avant* (front-wheel-drive) car.

COACH-BUILT bodies were constructed on a separate frame which was fitted to the chassis and covered in aluminium panels. These coach-builders are making the wooden framework.

1922 BROUGH SUPERIOR. Motorcycles could be custom-built to the highest standards. George Brough claimed to build the 'Rolls-Royce' of motorcycles and would tailor his machines to the customer's needs. They were usually powerful bikes with a large 1000cc V-twin engine and could reach 160 km/h .

1930

1935

1938

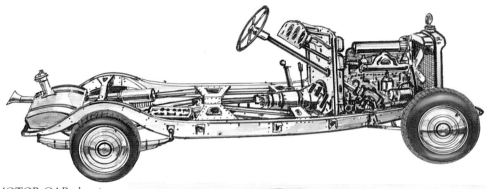

MOTOR CAR chassis, 1924. The chassis was made of U-section steel rails on which the engine, gearbox, springs and axles were mounted.

PRESSED STEEL BODY for the 1938 H-type Vauxhall. Instead of a separate body fixed to the chassis frames, the car was built as a rigid 'box' of welded steel parts which needed no separate chassis. The system started in the USA in 1916.

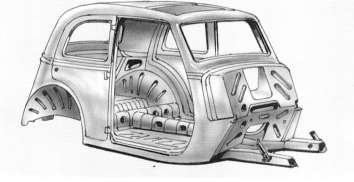

THE TOURING FACTORY in Milan, 1941. Car makers sent the finished chassis of their cars to coach-builders like Touring who fitted the hand-formed bodies.

ITALIAN ALFA ROMEO 8C of 1938, specially built for the Le Mans 24-hour race in northern France. The bodywork is by the Touring company of Milan, a specialist builder of lightweight bodies for high-performance cars.

1924 A *Boulogne* Hispano-Suiza. The Hispano-Suiza was the most fashionable of European cars. This powerful example, with an 8-litre engine, was raced by the French driver André Dubonnet in the Targa Florio race in Sicily.

1927 Bentley. W O Bentley (1888-1971) was a legend in his lifetime. He had designed aero engines during World War One and later built famous fast cars. Bentleys won the gruelling Le Mans 24-hour race five times, in 1924 and 1927-30. The race, which was first held in 1923, is still run on ordinary, public roads and continues to be one of the most prestigious events in motor-racing.

1930 Alfa Romeo 6C 1750 Gran Turismo. This confirmed Alfa as the leading Italian maker of high-performance cars. It was expensive, but enthusiasts found the top speed of 150 km/h was combined with exceptionally accurate steering and fine roadholding. Zagato of Milan built the most stylish bodies for Alfas.

1935 Bugatti Atlantic. The type 57S 3.3-litre twin-cam engine gave this Bugatti a top speed of about 180 km/h. The style reflected a growing interest in streamlining. The aerodynamic curves and the name hinted at an unusual blend of American and European aesthetics.

1938 Cadillac Sixty Special. The Cadillac was America's equivalent of the Rolls-Royce. However, the Rolls-Royce was largely hand-built, whereas the Cadillac relied on mass production and many machine-made parts.

1922   1923   1925

Cars For The People

Ad, c1933, showing the wind slowing a conventional saloon car compared to the streamlined Czech Tatra.

CHRYSLER AIRFLOW, 1934. In the USA, Walter Chrysler used the new streamlined look to boost sales of his cars. This style was unpopular at first, but soon all cars had a smooth rounded look.

As soon as cars were invented, makers such as De Dion and Renault produced small, cheaper models. But it was mainly the rich who wanted cars, and they also wanted comfort, speed and space, which meant big cars with large (and expensive) engines.

The first popular small cars were known as 'cyclecars' because they were lightweight and based on motorcycle engines and parts. Controls, such as the accelerator, could be a hand lever like a motorcycle's, and not a pedal on the floor. The position of the controls also varied from maker to maker – they were not standardized as they are today. Some buyers preferred a motorcycle for cheap transport, as they were often considerably more reliable than the 'cyclecars'.

The big change came with the British Austin Seven, introduced in 1922. It was designed like one of the big cars, with similar types of controls and could, at a pinch, seat four. Soon all major makers offered cheap cars and ownership increased rapidly. In Germany the Austin Seven was built under licence by Dixi, the predecessor of BMW, and in Japan by Datsun (now Nissan).

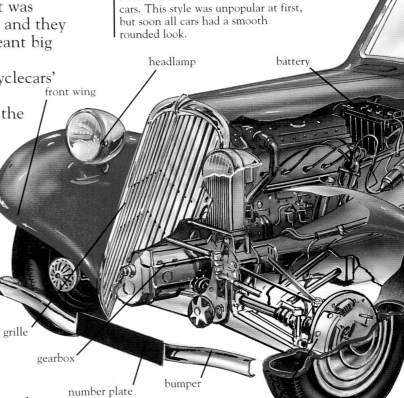

front wing

headlamp

battery

radiator grille

gearbox

number plate

bumper

front brakes

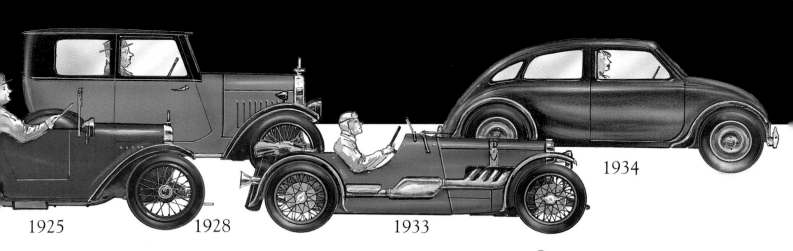

1925   1928   1933   1934

AUTO UNION, 1934. Volkswagen designer Ferdinand Porsche also designed this high-speed, supercharged 16-cylinder racer with 300hp and a top speed of 280 km/h.

windscreen wipers   sliding sunroof

leather upholstery

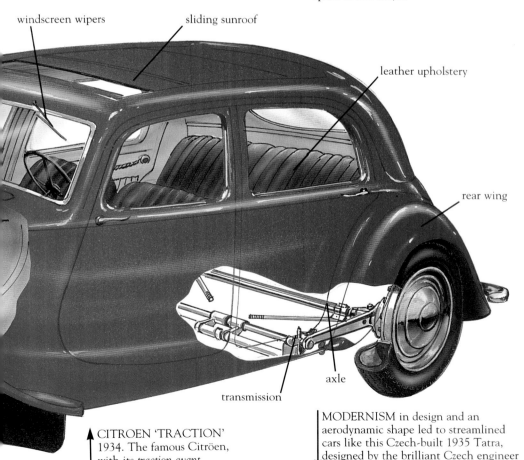

rear wing

axle

transmission

CITROEN 'TRACTION' 1934. The famous Citröen, with its *traction avant* front-wheel drive, became a most influential car.

MODERNISM in design and an aerodynamic shape led to streamlined cars like this Czech-built 1935 Tatra, designed by the brilliant Czech engineer Hans Ledwinka (1878–1967).

1922 Morgan three-wheeler. Like many small cars made in the years after World War One, this Morgan was very light. As a result it could reach speeds of 128 km/h, compared with the Austin Seven's 72 km/h.

1923 Motorcycle combination. In the early 1920s the cheapest motorized transport for a couple or small family was the motorcycle and sidecar, or 'combination'.

1925 Amilcar. France pioneered the popular small sports car, like this Amilcar. It only had a four-cylinder 1100cc engine, but the body was so light it was said to reach speeds of 120km/h.

1925 Austin Seven. The Austin Seven, introduced by Herbert Austin in 1922, was the first popular British car. At £100 the 1922 model was twice the price of a motorcycle combination, but it could take four adults in reasonable comfort.

1928 Morris Minor. Other manufacturers soon copied the Austin Seven formula. The Morris Minor was produced by William Morris (later Lord Nuffield).

1933 MG K3 Magnette. In Britain MGs were the most popular small sports cars. (MG stood for Morris Garages.) This supercharged K3 Magnette had great success both in racing and at speed hillclimbs against the clock.

1934 The prototype of the German Volkswagen (people's car) designed by Ferdinand Porsche, and nicknamed the 'Beetle'. Workers were meant to save for it by weekly payments.

1939   1939   1940

WORLD WAR TWO

The Welbike folding scooter was developed during World War Two. It was dropped with paratroops on its own parachute.

World War

Two (1939-45) was the first truly motorized war. In World War One (1914-18) trucks and cars had been used to some extent. But motor transport was not an essential part of the struggle.

In World War Two, German military planners were the first to realize how motorized transport could change warfare. They understood that trucks and cars would not simply be more convenient – they would allow a new kind of fast attack, the *Blitzkrieg*, to surprise the enemy. Instead of deadlocked lines of trenches with armies facing each other for years, as in World War One, tanks would smash through the enemy's defences, helped by aircraft, and motorized troops would pour through.

The USA, Britain, Germany and Russia used the full capacity of their motor industries for the war. In 1942 alone Britain made 160,000 trucks and imported another 190,000 from North America. Transporting petrol became as important as providing food and ammunition. It was so vital to have a tough, portable container for carrying petrol that a factory was set up in Britain specially to make a copy of the tough German 'jerrican' for the Allied forces.

IN 1943 the Jeep was converted into an amphibious vehicle. But it had a number of design faults and was little used.

BRITISH ARMY despatch riders disembarking in Normandy on D-Day, 6 June 1944. Nearly half a million motorcycles were made in Britain during the war for army use.

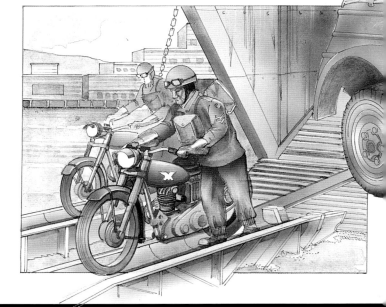

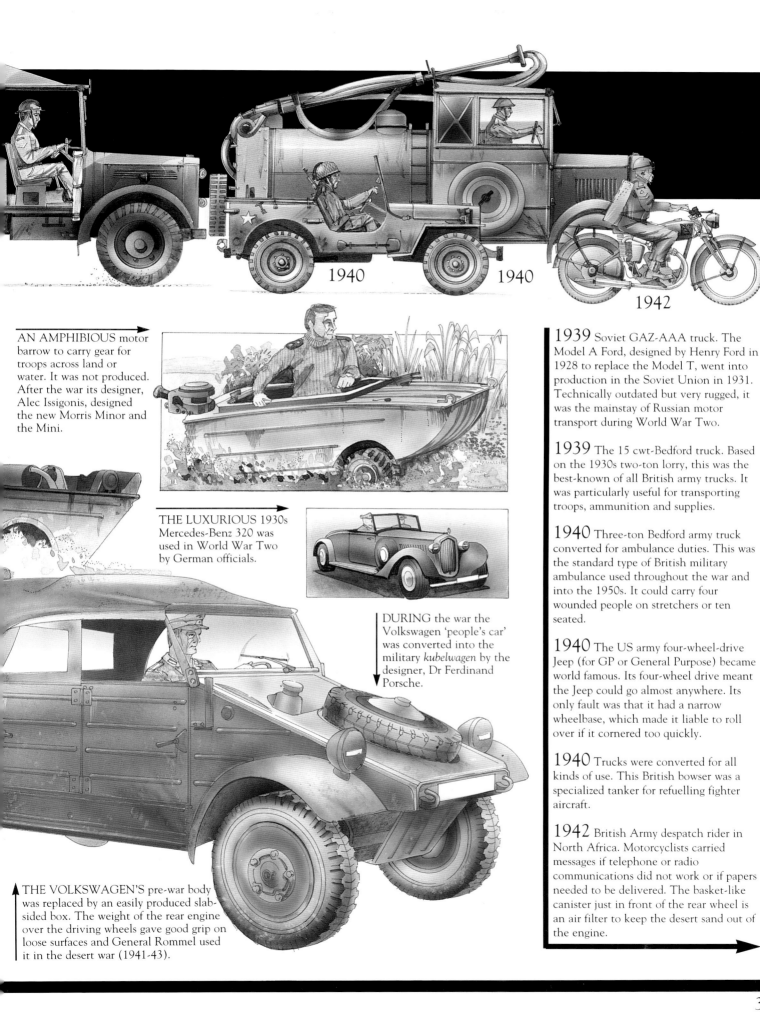

1940

1940

1942

AN AMPHIBIOUS motor barrow to carry gear for troops across land or water. It was not produced. After the war its designer, Alec Issigonis, designed the new Morris Minor and the Mini.

THE LUXURIOUS 1930s Mercedes-Benz 320 was used in World War Two by German officials.

DURING the war the Volkswagen 'people's car' was converted into the military *kubelwagen* by the designer, Dr Ferdinand Porsche.

THE VOLKSWAGEN'S pre-war body was replaced by an easily produced slab-sided box. The weight of the rear engine over the driving wheels gave good grip on loose surfaces and General Rommel used it in the desert war (1941-43).

1939 Soviet GAZ-AAA truck. The Model A Ford, designed by Henry Ford in 1928 to replace the Model T, went into production in the Soviet Union in 1931. Technically outdated but very rugged, it was the mainstay of Russian motor transport during World War Two.

1939 The 15 cwt-Bedford truck. Based on the 1930s two-ton lorry, this was the best-known of all British army trucks. It was particularly useful for transporting troops, ammunition and supplies.

1940 Three-ton Bedford army truck converted for ambulance duties. This was the standard type of British military ambulance used throughout the war and into the 1950s. It could carry four wounded people on stretchers or ten seated.

1940 The US army four-wheel-drive Jeep (for GP or General Purpose) became world famous. Its four-wheel drive meant the Jeep could go almost anywhere. Its only fault was that it had a narrow wheelbase, which made it liable to roll over if it cornered too quickly.

1940 Trucks were converted for all kinds of use. This British bowser was a specialized tanker for refuelling fighter aircraft.

1942 British Army despatch rider in North Africa. Motorcyclists carried messages if telephone or radio communications did not work or if papers needed to be delivered. The basket-like canister just in front of the rear wheel is an air filter to keep the desert sand out of the engine.

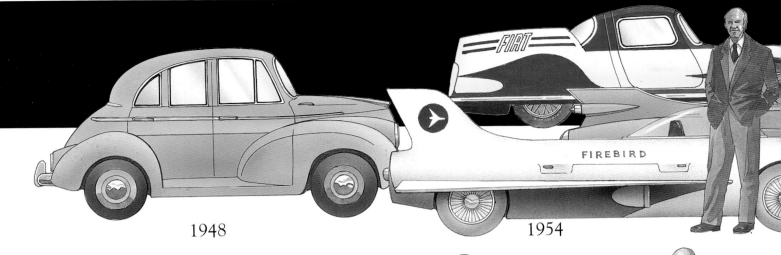

1948

1954

CARS WITH WINGS

Cycle motor, 1951. This tiny motor could be fitted to an ordinary bicycle to provide very cheap motor transport.

After World War Two the American economy boomed.

Production switched from tanks and planes to cars and fridges. Wages increased every year and this was reflected in the cars produced. Each year manufacturers brought out models that were bigger, flashier and more curvaceous than the one before.

At General Motors (GM), Harley Earl was in charge of styling. He had once built cars for Hollywood stars and claimed that design was an entertainment business. American jet planes were breaking the sound barrier, so Earl's special 'Firebird' show cars echoed their dash with wings and streamlining, which soon found their way onto the cars GM sold to the public.

In other countries times were tougher. Economy was essential so cars were small, though they might imitate US styling. Many people used a bike with a tiny cycle motor. In Italy the scooter was devised as popular transport. In Japan Soichiro Honda introduced a 50cc economy model. In time, this was to prove the spearhead of Japan's invasion of the world's vehicle markets.

IN 1946 the Italian company, Vespa, invented the step-through scooter. The new machines were clean, simple to operate and had enclosed engines, unlike traditional motorcycles. The metal leg shield and footrest also meant that people using them for short city journeys did not have to wear protective clothing.

SOICHIRO HONDA changed the face of motorcycling with his new lightweight Honda 50, launched in 1958.

whitewall tyres

1948 PONTIAC Silver Streak. In the USA after World War Two cars were big and comfortable, with rounded, pre-war aerodynamic styling. But soon American cars were to echo new trends in aviation.

chrome fittings

Silver Streak logo

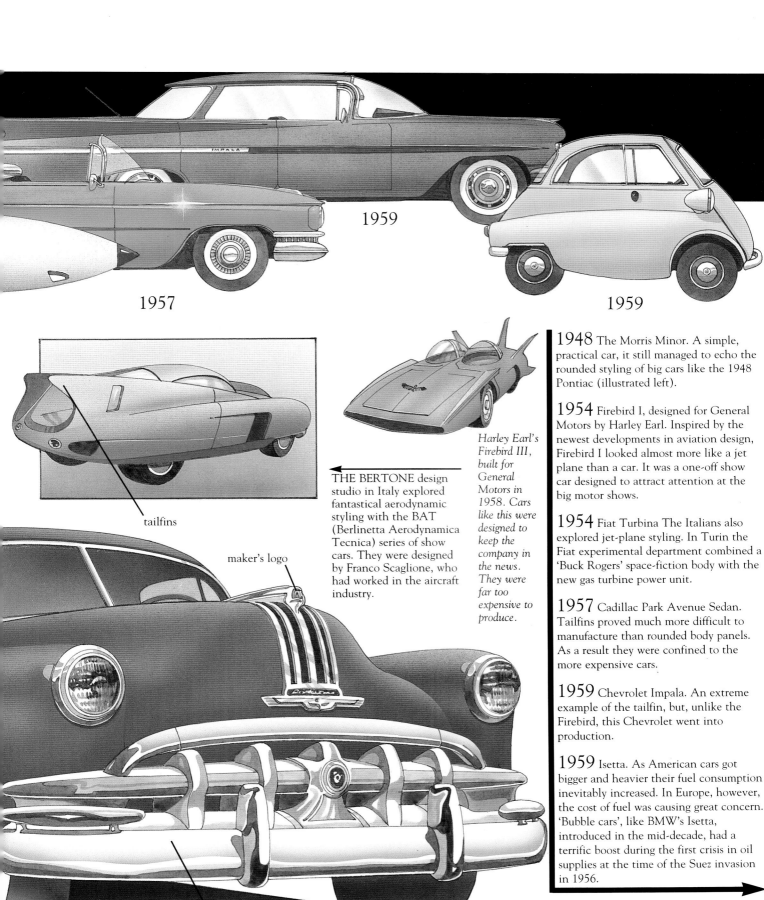

1959

1957

1959

tailfins

maker's logo

chrome bumper

THE BERTONE design studio in Italy explored fantastical aerodynamic styling with the BAT (Berlinetta Aerodynamica Tecnica) series of show cars. They were designed by Franco Scaglione, who had worked in the aircraft industry.

Harley Earl's Firebird III, built for General Motors in 1958. Cars like this were designed to keep the company in the news. They were far too expensive to produce.

1948 The Morris Minor. A simple, practical car, it still managed to echo the rounded styling of big cars like the 1948 Pontiac (illustrated left).

1954 Firebird I, designed for General Motors by Harley Earl. Inspired by the newest developments in aviation design, Firebird I looked almost more like a jet plane than a car. It was a one-off show car designed to attract attention at the big motor shows.

1954 Fiat Turbina The Italians also explored jet-plane styling. In Turin the Fiat experimental department combined a 'Buck Rogers' space-fiction body with the new gas turbine power unit.

1957 Cadillac Park Avenue Sedan. Tailfins proved much more difficult to manufacture than rounded body panels. As a result they were confined to the more expensive cars.

1959 Chevrolet Impala. An extreme example of the tailfin, but, unlike the Firebird, this Chevrolet went into production.

1959 Isetta. As American cars got bigger and heavier their fuel consumption inevitably increased. In Europe, however, the cost of fuel was causing great concern. 'Bubble cars', like BMW's Isetta, introduced in the mid-decade, had a terrific boost during the first crisis in oil supplies at the time of the Suez invasion in 1956.

1949   1958   1958

MINIS AND SUPERMINIS

*Alec Issigonis (1906-1988),
the influential designer of the
Morris Minor and the Mini.*

The Mini, designed by Alec Issigonis, was launched in 1959. Front-wheel drive and a transverse engine (one placed sideways across the car) squeezed the mechanical parts into the smallest possible space. As a result, the tiny Mini provided comfort for four adults and the same performance as a much larger car.

Eventually all the big European car makers designed their own front-engined front-wheel-drive 'minis'. The unified engine, gearbox and drive combined under the bonnet was more costly to design and build than the older rear-wheel-drive types. However, the extra room it provided brought extra sales, so making the cost worthwhile. Volkswagen, desperate to find a replacement for the dated Beetle, scored a real hit with its successor, the Golf, designed by the famous Turin designer Giorgetto Giugiaro.

Meanwhile, imports from Japan were starting to take a share of the European car market. In 1956 Japanese car makers produced 32,000 cars. In 1993 they made over 8 million, of which half were exported. Throughout the 1980s, Japanese cars took an increasing share of the market for standard cars. Then, in the 1990s, they entered the luxury car market, challenging makers such as Mercedes, Jaguar and BMW.

THE 'REVOLUTIONARY' Mini was manufactured on a traditional moving assembly line of the type pioneered by Henry Ford before World War One.

FOR MOTOR SHOW displays a Mini was cut in half to show just how well all the space was used.

rear-view mirror

engine positioned across the car

radiator

hub cap

gear lever

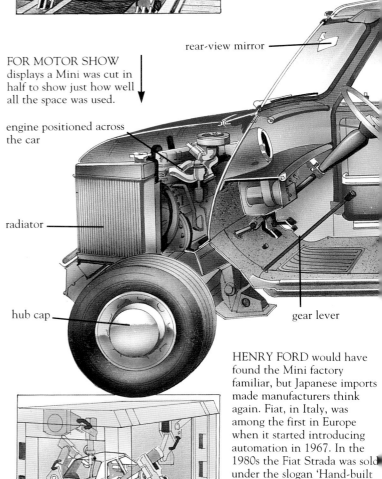

HENRY FORD would have found the Mini factory familiar, but Japanese imports made manufacturers think again. Fiat, in Italy, was among the first in Europe when it started introducing automation in 1967. In the 1980s the Fiat Strada was sold under the slogan 'Hand-built by Robots'.

1974   1974   1983

THE JAPANESE car export boom. Toyota Corollas waiting to be loaded for export in 1974. The cars were often exported in the car makers' own ships.

sliding window

shelf behind rear seat for small items

boot

spare wheel

exhaust

wheels only 25cm in diameter help save space in body of car

handbrake

felt underlay to help soundproofing

BY THE 1980s cars in the Fiat factories were carried from point to point on self-guided pallets. These moved around automatically, reversing in and out of machines according to the work sequence and the model they carried.

1949 Bond Minicar. European economies were still strained after World War Two, so ultra-cheap cars were popular. The basic Bond had a single front wheel driven by a simple, two-stroke motorcycle engine.

1958 Messerschmitt Tiger. This was the best made and most popular of all the bubble cars. Introduced in 1953, it went out of production in 1962.

1958 Mini prototype. Just as the Austin Seven had triumphed over the cyclecars in 1922, Alec Issigonis intended his new 'Mini' to capture the market occupied by the various economy vehicles and bubble cars.

1974 The Volkswagen Golf, designed by Giorgetto Giugiaro. Like the Mini it had front-wheel drive with a transverse engine. It became one of the most successful cars of all time. Introduced in 1974, by 1988 it had sold 10 million. By 1993 total sales throughout the world were 145 million.

1974 The Toyota Corolla was typical of the Japanese cars that emerged in the late 1960s and early 1970s. Unsophisticated, both mechanically and in their design, they were nevertheless cheap and reliable.

1983 The Fiat Unò, also designed by Giorgetto Giugiaro, followed the Mini principle. But four extra centimetres of roof height gave it a much greater feeling of space than its rivals the Mini, Metro, Renault 5, Golf or Peugeot 104. It became Fiat's best selling car.

1966   1967

REVOLUTIONARY DESIGNS

Felix Wankel (1902-88). Designs for his revolutionary new engine were bought by car makers throughout the world.

In 1966 a new engine was introduced – the Wankel rotary. It was smooth and almost without vibration. It was also half the size of traditional engines of similar power, so a car's passenger space could be larger.

The German engineer Felix Wankel (1902-88) had dreamed for years of devising a new, smoother-running form of engine. His design had a triangular rotor which both spun round and at the same time 'waltzed' around inside a specially shaped chamber, replacing the up-and-down piston of the traditional engine. The German NSU company began building it, but problems with the Wankel's reliability started to give it a bad reputation. By the time the company got the engine right in the 1970s, fuel prices were rising and the thirsty Wankel was dropped.

The real revolutions in the car were less dramatic – but more profound. During the 1960s more and more attention was given to the whole design. Crash testing, stimulated mainly by the rise of consumer power in the USA, forced all car makers to consider safety more seriously. At the same time rising oil prices meant governments and car owners wanted better fuel consumption.

AN EXECUTIVE at Chrysler, one of the USA's 'big three' car makers, called the Wankel engine 'the most unbelievable fantasy'.

twin rear-view mirrors

speedometer and rev counter

headlight

shock absorbers

mudguard support

wheel spokes

front brakes

exhaust pipe

Computer-aided design (CAD) was used first by the aerospace industry in the early 1960s. By the late 1960s car makers, appreciating the speed and accuracy of its design predictions, were using it too.

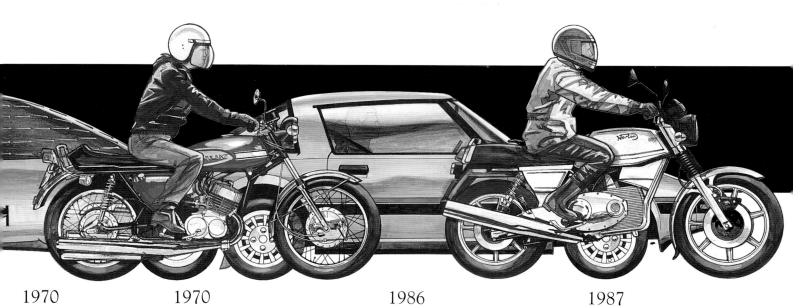

1970   1970   1986   1987

UNTIL CRASH TESTS
started in the 1960s,
designers had little idea
what happened to
occupants in a real crash.
Here a Volvo is
undergoing a crash test.

1966 The NSU Spyder was offered for
sale with an optional Wankel rotary
engine. In 1967 it won the small sports
car class in the German hillclimb
championships.

1967 The NSU Ro 80 was voted Car
of the Year. The Wankel engine made it
smoother to drive than other cars on the
market, but the engine kept wearing out,
making it both expensive and
impractical.

1970 Testing an experimental car in
the Pininfarina wind tunnel, Turin, Italy.
The real revolution in car design did not
come from a single invention like the
Wankel, but a combination of computer
modelling and design, aerodynamics and
crash research.

1970 A two-stroke Kawasaki 500cc
motorbike. In contrast to the four-
cylinder Honda (left) which had gone on
sale the previous year, the Kawasaki was
mechanically crude. However, it was
cheap and excitingly powerful.

1986 Mazda RX 7 sports car. Only the
Japanese Mazda company persevered with
the Wankel rotary engine. Eventually
they overcame the problems, but the car
sells only to enthusiasts who like sports
cars with unusual engines.

1987 Norton Rotary. The Norton
motorcycle company has used the rotary
engine since 1969. To date they have
sold only about 950.

maker's name

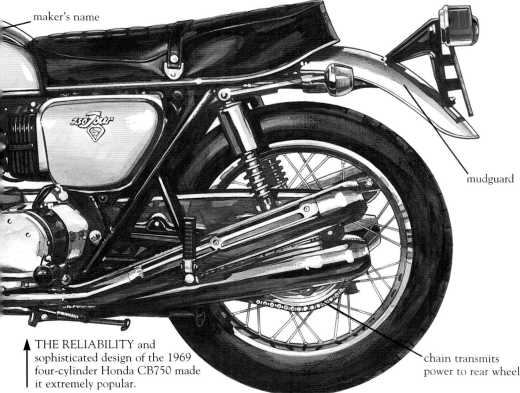

mudguard

chain transmits
power to rear wheel

THE RELIABILITY and
sophisticated design of the 1969
four-cylinder Honda CB750 made
it extremely popular.

*Computers allow designers to juggle all the variables to meet
targets for roominess, performance, fuel consumption and
crash resistance without building several expensive prototypes
before a new model goes into production.*

*When the new car's design
is fixed, the computer can
program the machine tools
to form the car parts.*

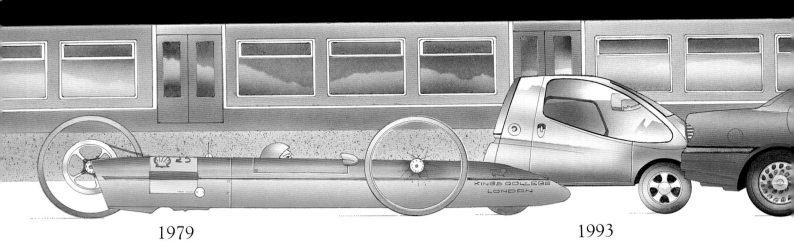

1979

1993

THE PRESENT DAY

In California, off-road trail-riding produced the mountain bike: a heavier bike with chunky tyres.

Many people think that private, car-borne transport is in crisis. Environmentalists blame the car for global warming, through its emission of carbon dioxide. In some cities, such as Los Angeles and Athens, where there is little wind and exhaust gases reach dangerous levels, governments now set very low legal limits for emissions.

Electric cars are favoured by many, although they still cause pollution – at the power station. Other suggestions include hybrid electric/diesel units, alcohol-burning engines and auxiliary solar power. None of these tackle the problem of congestion – only leaving the car at home will do that.

However, with cities and communities built the way they are now, for many people the car is the most convenient form of transport. Better, more flexible public transport and revolutionary changes to work patterns and the structure of communities will probably be needed before people can be persuaded to give up their cars.

Will the growing use of electronic communications and computers produce more 'networking' – working from home and keeping in touch by telecommunications 'superhighways'? What will the future bring? That depends partly on what *you* choose.

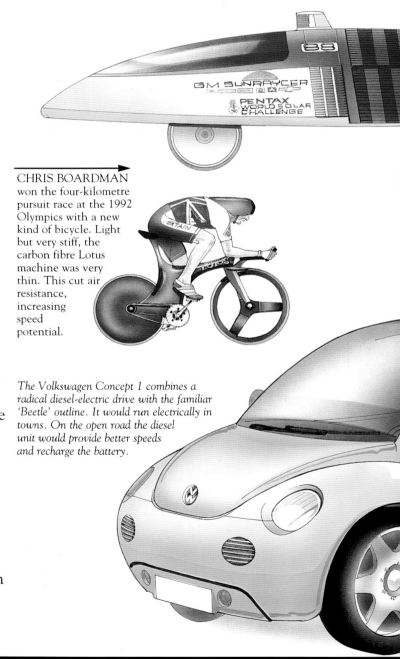

CHRIS BOARDMAN won the four-kilometre pursuit race at the 1992 Olympics with a new kind of bicycle. Light but very stiff, the carbon fibre Lotus machine was very thin. This cut air resistance, increasing speed potential.

The Volkswagen Concept 1 combines a radical diesel-electric drive with the familiar 'Beetle' outline. It would run electrically in towns. On the open road the diesel unit would provide better speeds and recharge the battery.

1993   1994   1999?

IN THE USA AND AUSTRALIA there are regular solar-power races. The General Motors Sunrayer won the 1987 Darwin to Sydney race at an average speed of 67 km/h (42 mph).

THE SURFACE OF THE SUNRAYCER is covered with silicon solar cells. It carries one person and runs on about 1000 watts – the same as a domestic hairdryer.

HARLEY-DAVIDSON motorcycle, 1994. The Harley-Davidson recalls the original V-twin-engined machines that became a cult with American bikers in the 1950s.

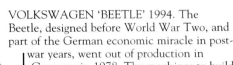

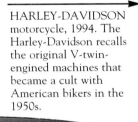

VOLKSWAGEN 'BEETLE' 1994. The Beetle, designed before World War Two, and part of the German economic miracle in post-war years, went out of production in Germany in 1978. The machines to build it were shipped to Brazil where it is still made.

1979 King's College Mileage Marathon Car. The 'Mileage Marathon' is a regular UK motor sport event for university engineering departments, schools and car companies to show what fuel economy can be achieved. With a tiny engine and a pencil-thin body, this experimental lightweight (40-kilo) car did 640 km per litre. The latest designs can do more than 1,200 km per litre.

1987 Docklands Light Railway. Not so much a railway, more a lift on its side, the transport system installed for London's Docklands uses driverless coaches controlled by computer.

1993 IDEA electric car. The electric car has been seen as the solution to city traffic problems. Will this snappy two-seater from the Turin design house IDEA be the first practical electric town car?

1993 Ford Mondeo 'World Car'. For years the world's big car makers dreamed of huge economies if they could make one car to suit users in many countries. The Mondeo is the first example.

1994 Bugatti EB 110. In spite of the economic recession that began in the late 1980s and the 'Green' conservation movement, there are still people who want supercars like this 550bhp four-wheel-drive turbocharged Bugatti. It can do 320 km/h.

1999? Vehicles with internal combustion engines are not the only wheeled transport. Bangladeshi rickshaw drivers pedal customers around town in environmentally friendly rickshaws.

TRANSPORT FACTS

The ox is the earliest known draught animal.

Horse-drawn chariots were first used in Egypt around 1600 BC.

The first postal service may be that referred to in the Bible's Old Testament Book of Ezra, which states that letters were sent 'by post on horseback and riders on mules, camels and young dromedaries'.

Most examples of early wheeled vehicles come from tombs in the Middle East, Russia and Europe. Wheeled vehicles were so rare and special that kings and princes were buried with them.

From AD 43 the Romans built an 8,000-kilometre road network in Britain in just 40 years.

In Tibet, the yak is the principal form of transport.

Horses were never a cheap form of transport. Their working life was short and each horse ate the produce of 2.5 hectares of farmland each year.

The first self-propelled vehicle, Nicholas Cugnot's steamer, made a run in Paris in 1769 and hit a wall.

In the most prosperous parts of Europe in the late 18th century there were almost four carts or waggons and six horses for every ten households – a figure very similar to the number of cars owned by people living in the countryside until around the beginning of the 1960s.

In 1811 in Britain half a million horses were used just for transport. Ninety years later, in 1901, the figure was 1.7 million.

By 1836, the best mail coaches could average 16-17 km/h. To achieve these speeds the horses pulling them were changed every 13 kilometres.

J.B. Dunlop invented the pneumatic tyre in 1888. It was first used on bicycles.

A Panhard won the first road race, from Paris to Bordeaux and back again, in 1895. Driven by Emile Levassor, the distance of 1,178 kilometres was covered in two days.

By the second half of the 19th century the widespread railway network meant that country roads throughout Europe were all but abandoned, used by a few village carts, farm waggons and gentlemen driving themselves in dog carts. Into this forgotten world cyclists arrived like explorers.

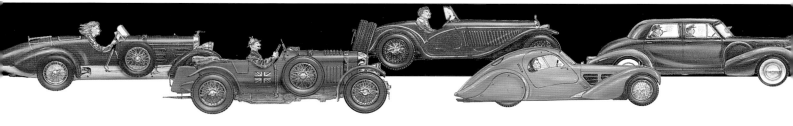

In the USA the new-fangled bicycle was much appreciated. 'It takes men out of the bar-rooms into the pure air' wrote one commentator. 'Walking is obsolete', claimed the *Scientific American*.

Roller-skates (called wheel-skates) were invented in the 19th century as a new form of sport.

The name Mercedes was used for the first time on Daimler cars in 1900. A wealthy Frenchman ordered 30 cars and demanded that, in return, the cars should be called after his daughter.

Dust was one of the greatest problems brought by the early motor car. The solution was the 'Tarmac' road surface – a mixture of small stones and asphalt, invented by a Nottingham county surveyor in 1902.

In the early years of motoring, motor cycles were more numerous than cars. In 1904 Britain had 16,000 motor bikes and only 14,000 cars.

In 1903 Henry Ford founded the Ford motor company.

In 1911 Cadillac became the first company to offer electric starting and lights as standard fittings in its cars.

In 1913 nearly 90% of goods were still transported by horse-drawn vehicles in industrialized countries.

In the early years of motoring there were no garages. Car-owners had to buy petrol for their cars at chemists or hardware stores.

The American 1940 Oldsmobile was the first car to have a fully automatic gearbox.

The invention of the gas turbine (jet) in World War Two made people think the new engine would soon be found in all kinds of vehicles. The first experimental gas turbine car, Rover's JET 1, ran in 1950 but a gas turbine car has poor fuel economy and has still not been made for sale.

The American car industry made its 200 millionth automobile in 1966, seventy years after Henry Ford built his first car.

In 1965 the publication of *Unsafe at any speed* by the American, Ralph Nader, revolutionized public attitudes to car safety. Crash testing of cars was one result.

Next to the car, the shopping trolley is the most common four-wheeled 'vehicle' in the world today.

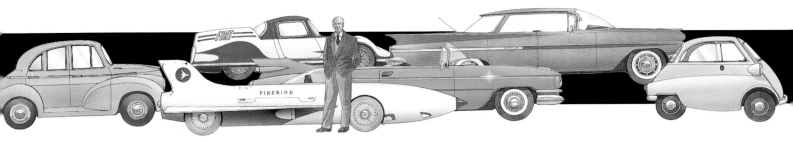

GLOSSARY

Aerodynamics The study of air flow and air behaviour. Applied to cars, it can reduce fuel consumption and increase stability.

Air-cooled Petrol engines when running give out heat and burn fuel. They must be kept cool so that the metal parts do not overheat and seize up. In air-cooled vehicles this is achieved by a current of air passing over a finned surface in the engine.

Axle The shaft or beam that joins a pair of wheels.

Camshaft A rotating shaft with lobes that work the inlet and exhaust valves in a four-stroke engine.

Catalyst In a car, a device fitted in the exhaust to absorb emissions from the burning of the fuel, whether petrol or diesel.

Chassis The steel frame on which early cars were built.

Chrome/chromium A hard metal that does not corrode. Since the 1930s a thin layer of chromium (chromium plate) has been used over steel parts to improve the appearance of 'trim' and components like bumpers. Before that nickel plating was used.

Crash test A test in which a real car is accelerated into a concrete barrier. Instruments and dummies are used to measure how well or badly occupants would have been protected if it had been a real crash. As a result of such tests, the vehicle's design may be modified.

Cylinder The part of the engine where the fuel and air burns, driving down the piston that fits inside it. Some small motorcycles have one cylinder. Most popular cars have four.

Emissions Chemical pollutants, such as oxides of nitrogen, that occur in engine exhaust gases.

Horsepower (hp) Unit for measuring the power of an engine. James Watt (1736-1819), the steam engine builder, was the first to work out a figure for comparison. Today, engine power is more often measured in kilowatts: 1 hp = 0.745 kW

Mass production The technique of making things in large numbers, so making them cheaper.

Magneto Type of engine-driven dynamo that produces a high voltage spark to fire the fuel/air mixture in the engine at each revolution.

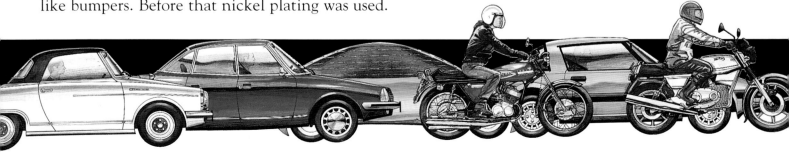

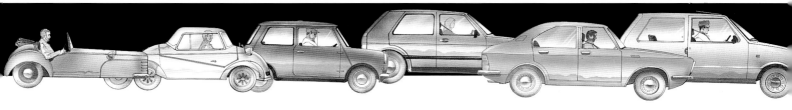

Panel beating The art of forming sheet metal (usually aluminium) with special hammers and hand tools to make car body parts. All veteran and vintage cars were made in this way.

Postillion Person controlling a coach or cart by riding on one of the horses pulling it, rather than on the vehicle itself.

Pressed steel Sheet steel pressed into special forms by powerful tools called presses. The parts in the press which form the steel to the chosen shape are called dies.

Shafts The horizontal poles on a coach or cart between which the horse stands. The poles support the collar that the horse pulls on.

Speed hillclimb A competitive event in which cars run singly against the clock up a twisting hill road. It was very popular in the 1920s and 1930s.

Sprocket Special gear-like wheel with teeth to fit a special chain. Used in bicycles, motorcycles and many other machines.

Stage coach A coach that travelled in 'stages' so that the horses could be changed at planned stops for fresh ones. In this way the speed of coach travel could be improved.

Styling Designing the appearance of cars. The styling studios used to make models with clay, just like sculptors. Today much of the work is done with computers.

Supercharger An engine-driven air-pump which forces extra air into an engine and increases its power.

Toll road Road where a charge is made for using it. First introduced in Europe in the 18th century to raise money for road repairs, tolls still have to be paid for using many European motorways and bridges.

Transmission The gears and shafts that connect the engine to the driving wheels of a car or truck.

Travois Sliding wheelless load carrier made of two pieces of wood and designed to be pulled by an animal. The animal can transport a greater weight than if the whole load was on its back.

Turbocharger A pump to provide an engine with extra air, like a supercharger but driven by the exhaust gas and not by the engine.

Twin-cam An engine with two camshafts in the cylinder head to work the valves. Often used for high performance cars.

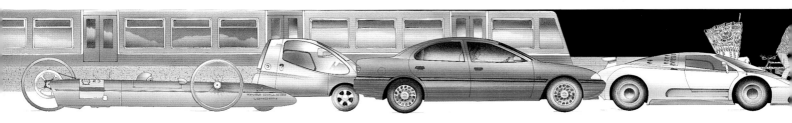

INDEX